Copyright ©DAVE WHITFIELD RND 2021

All rights reserved. No part of this publication may be reproduced, distributed, or transmitted in any form or by any means, including photocopying, recording, or other electronic or mechanical methods, without the prior written permission of the publisher, except in the case of brief quotations embodied in critical reviews and certain other noncommercial uses permitted by copyright law

Contents

INTRODUCTION 4
What Is the Sirtfood Diet? 5
   Is It Healthy and Sustainable? 14
GETTING STARTED 18
   THE HEALTH BENEFITS 19
   GETTING ENOUGH SIRTS 22
   Sirtfood Diet And Exercise 24
   The Sirt Diet Principles 25
   Once the diet becomes a way of life 27
   Spice Up Your Sirtfood Diet With Bird's-Eye Chilies . 29
   Drinking Green Tea 31
   What Are The Best Juicers? 34
   Masticating Juicers 36
   Here is the complete range of the Green Star Juicers at Amazon. 40
Here are the top 5 foods for Sirt diet 43
New Sirtfood Recipes 46
   Moroccan Spiced Eggs-New Sirtfood Recipes 61
   Fresh Saag Paneer-New Sirtfood Recipes 71
   Mocha Chocolate Mousse-New Sirtfood Recipes new sirtfood recipes 74
   Buckwheat Superfood Muesli -New Sirtfood Recipes new sirtfood recipes 76

For the Blueberry Banana Pancakes 81

For the Blueberry Banana Pancakes 82

Sirt Chilli Con Carne-New Sirtfood Recipes new sirtfood recipes 89

ASIAN KING PRAWN STIR-FRY WITH BUCKWHEAT NOODLES –SIRTFOOD RECIPESsirtfood recipes 101

sirtfood recipesCHOC CHIP GRANOLA-SIRTFOOD RECIPES 106

LAMB,BUTTERNUT SQUASH AND DATE TAGINE-SIRTFOOD RECIPES 111

PRAWN ARRABBIATA-SIRTFOOD RECIPES sirtfood recipes 115

BAKED POTATOES WITH SPICY CHICKPEA STEW-SIRTFOOD RECIPESsirtfood recipes 123

sirtfood recipesGRAPE AND MELON JUICE-SIRTFOOD RECIPES 127

sirtfood recipes 131

KALE AND BLACKCURRANT SMOOTHIE-SIRTFOOD RECIPES 134

KALE, EDAMAME AND TOFU CURRY-SIRTFOOD RECIPES sirtfood recipes 140

CONCLUSION 148

INTRODUCTION

Trendy new diets seem to pop up regularly, and the Sirtfood Diet is one of the latest. It has become a favorite of celebrities in Europe and is famous for allowing red wine and chocolate. Its creators insist that it's not a fad, but rather that "sirtfoods" are the secret to unlocking fat loss and preventing disease. However, health experts warn that this diet may not live up to the hype and could even be a bad idea. This article provides an evidence-based review of the Sirtfood Diet and its potential health benefits.

What Is the Sirtfood Diet?

The Sirtfood Diet is the new way to shift weight quickly without radical dieting by activating the same 'skinny gene' pathways usually just induced by exercise and fasting. Certain foods contain chemicals called polyphenols that put mild stress on our cells, turning on genes that mimic the effects of fasting and exercise. Foods rich in polyphenols-including kale, dark chocolate and red wine-trigger the sirtuin pathways that impact metabolism, aging and mood. A diet rich in these sirtfoods kick-starts weight loss without sacrificing muscle, while maintaining optimal health.

Add healthy sirtfoods to your diet for effective and sustained weight loss, incredible energy and glowing health. Switch on your body's fat-burning powers, supercharge weight loss and help stave off disease with this easy-to-follow diet developed by the experts in nutritional medicine who proved the impact of sirtfoods. Dark chocolate, coffee, kale – these are all foods that activate sirtuins and switch on the so-called 'skinny gene' pathways in the body. The Sirtfood Diet gives you a simple, healthy way of eating for weight loss, delicious easy-to-make recipes and a maintenance plan for prolonged success. The Sirtfood Diet is a diet of inclusion not exclusion, and sirtfoods are widely available and affordable. This is a diet that encourages you to pick up your knife and fork, and enjoy eating delicious healthy food while seeing the health and weight-loss benefits.

How to Follow the Sirtfood Diet

The Sirtfood Diet has two phases that last a total of three weeks. After that, you can continue "sirtifying" your diet by including as many sirtfoods as possible in your meals. The specific recipes for these two phases are found in

The Sirtfood Diet book, which was written by the diet's creators. You'll need to purchase it to follow the diet. The meals are full of sirtfoods but do include other ingredients besides just the "top 20 sirtfoods." Most of the ingredients and sirtfoods are easy to find. However, three of the signature ingredients required for these two phases — matcha green tea powder, lovage and buckwheat — may be expensive or difficult to find. A big part of the diet is its green juice, which you'll need to make yourself between one and three times daily. You will need a juicer (a blender will not work) and a kitchen scale, as the ingredients are listed by weight. The recipe is below:

• Sirtfood Green Juice

• 75 grams (2.5 oz) kale

• 30 grams (1 oz) arugula (rocket)

- 5 grams parsley

- 2 celery sticks

- 1 cm (0.5 in) ginger

- half a green apple

- half a lemon

- half a teaspoon matcha green tea

Juice all ingredients except for the green tea powder and lemon together, and pour them into a glass. Juice the lemon by hand, then stir both the lemon juice and green tea powder into your juice.

Phase One

The first phase lasts seven days and involves calorie restriction and lots of green juice. It is intended to jump-start your weight loss and claimed to help you lose 7 pounds (3.2 kg) in seven days. During the first three days of phase one, calorie intake is restricted to 1,000 calories. You drink three green juices per day plus one meal. Each day you can choose from recipes in the book, which all involve sirtfoods as a main part of the meal. Meal examples include miso-glazed tofu, the sirtfood omelet or a shrimp stir-fry with buckwheat noodles. On days 4–7 of phase one, calorie intake is increased to 1,500. This includes two green juices per day and two more sirtfood-rich meals, which you can choose from the book.

Phase Two

Phase two lasts for two weeks. During this "maintenance" phase, you should continue to steadily lose weight. There is no specific calorie limit for this phase. Instead, you eat three meals full of sirtfoods and one green juice per day. Again, the meals are chosen from recipes provided in the book.

After the Diet

You may repeat these two phases as often as desired for further weight loss. However, you are encouraged to continue "sirtifying" your diet after completing these phases by incorporating sirtfoods regularly into your meals. There are a variety of Sirtfood Diet books that are full of recipes rich in sirtfoods. You can also include sirtfoods in your diet as a snack or in recipes you already use. Additionally, you are encouraged to continue drinking the green juice every day. In this way, the Sirtfood Diet becomes more of a lifestyle change than a one-time diet.

SUMMARY:

The Sirtfood Diet consists of two phases. Phase one lasts seven days and combines calorie restriction and green juices. Phase two lasts two weeks and includes three meals and one juice.

Are Sirtfoods the New Superfoods? There's no denying that sirtfoods are good for you. They are often high in nutrients and full of healthy plant compounds. Moreover, studies have associated many of the foods recommended on the Sirtfood Diet with health benefits.

For example, eating moderate amounts of dark chocolate with a high cocoa content may lower the risk of heart disease and help fight inflammation. Drinking green tea may reduce the risk of stroke and diabetes and help lower blood pressure. And turmeric has anti-inflammatory properties that have beneficial effects on the body in general and may even protect against chronic, inflammation-related diseases. In fact, the majority of sirtfoods have demonstrated health benefits in humans. However, evidence on the health benefits of increasing sirtuin protein levels is preliminary. Yet, research in animals and cell lines have shown exciting results. For example, researchers have found that increased levels of certain sirtuin proteins lead to longer lifespan in yeast, worms and mice. And during fasting or calorie restriction, sirtuin proteins tell the body to burn more fat for energy and improve insulin sensitivity. One study in mice found that increased sirtuin levels led to fat loss.

Some evidence suggests that sirtuins may also play a role in reducing inflammation, inhibiting the development of tumors and slowing the development of heart disease and Alzheimer's. While studies in mice and human cell lines have shown positive results, there have been no human studies examining the effects of increasing sirtuin levels. Therefore, whether increasing sirtuin protein levels in the body will lead to longer lifespan or a lower risk of cancer in humans is unknown. Research is currently underway to develop compounds effective at increasing sirtuin levels in the body. This way, human studies can begin to examine the effects of sirtuins on human health. Until then, it's not possible to determine the effects of increased sirtuin levels.

SUMMARY:

Sirtfoods are typically healthy foods. However, very little is known about how these foods affect sirtuin levels and human health.

Is It Healthy and Sustainable?

Sirtfoods are almost all healthy choices and may even result in some health benefits due to their antioxidant or anti-inflammatory properties.

Yet eating just a handful of particularly healthy foods cannot meet all of your body's nutritional needs.

The Sirtfood Diet is unnecessarily restrictive and offers no clear, unique health benefits over any other type of diet.

Furthermore, eating only 1,000 calories is typically not recommended without the supervision of a physician. Even eating 1,500 calories per day is excessively restrictive for many people. The diet also requires drinking up to three green juices per day. Although juices can be a good source of vitamins and minerals, they are also a source of sugar and contain almost none of the healthy fiber that whole fruits and vegetables do. What's more, sipping on juice throughout the whole day is a bad idea for both your blood sugar and your teeth.

Not to mention, because the diet is so limited in calories and food choice, it is more than likely deficient in protein, vitamins and minerals, especially during the first phase. Due to the low calorie levels and restrictive food choices, this diet may be difficult to stick to for the entire three weeks. Add that to the high initial costs of having to purchase a juicer, the book and certain rare and expensive ingredients, as well as the time costs of preparing specific meals and juices, and this diet becomes unfeasible and unsustainable for many people.

SUMMARY:

The Sirtfood Diet promotes healthy foods but is restrictive in calories and food choices. It also involves drinking lots of juice, which isn't a healthy recommendation.

Safety and Side Effects

Although the first phase of the Sirtfood Diet is very low in calories and nutritionally incomplete, there are no real safety concerns for the average, healthy adult considering the diet's short duration. Yet for someone with diabetes, calorie restriction and drinking mostly juice for the first few days of the diet may cause dangerous changes in blood sugar levels. Nevertheless, even a healthy person may experience some side effects — mainly hunger. Eating only 1,000–1,500 calories per day will leave just about anyone feeling hungry, especially if much of what you're consuming is juice, which is low in fiber, a nutrient that helps keep you feeling full. During phase one, you might experience other side effects such as fatigue, lightheadedness and irritability due to the calorie restriction. For the otherwise healthy adult, serious health consequences are unlikely if the diet is followed for only three weeks.

SUMMARY:

The Sirtfood Diet is low in calories and phase one is not nutritionally balanced. It may leave you hungry, but it's not dangerous for the average healthy adult.

GETTING STARTED

Daily juices are essential to the Sirtfood Diet. So make sure you have a juicer. You'll also need three key ingredients. Matcha is a powdered green tea and an important ingredient in the green juices. It's readily available online, if your local health food shop doesn't stock it. Similarly, lovage – a herb in the green juice recipe – can sometimes seem hard to find. But it's easy to buy seeds online to grow it in a pot on a windowsill. Finally, buckwheat. It's a fantastic alternative to more common grains, but most supermarkets mix buckwheat and wheat in their products. You're more likely to find 100 per cent buckwheat products in your local health food store. MEAL IDEAS For breakfast, try soy yogurt with mixed berries, chopped walnuts and dark chocolate, or for something savoury, an omelet packed with bacon, red chicory and parsley. The sirtfood salad is great for lunch – but if you're craving some carbs, a wholemeal pitta stuffed with turkey, cheese or hummus is healthy and filling. Dinnertime doesn't have to be dull, either: stir-fried prawns with kale and buckwheat noodles is a tasty evening meal. And, believe it or not, pizza is still on the menu if it's made the sirtfood way.

THE HEALTH BENEFITS

There is growing evidence that sirtuin activators may have a wide range of health benefits as well as building muscle and suppressing appetite. These include improving memory, helping the body better control blood sugar levels and cleaning up the damage from free radical molecules that can accumulate in cells and lead to cancer and other diseases.

'Substantial observational evidence exists for the beneficial effects of the intake of food and drinks rich in sirtuin activators in decreasing risks of chronic disease,' said Professor Frank Hu, an expert in nutrition and epidemiology at Harvard University in a recent article in the journal Advances In Nutrition. A sirtfood diet is particularly suitable as an anti-aging regime. Although sirtuin activators are found all through the plant kingdom, only certain fruits and vegetables have large enough amounts to count as sirtfoods. Examples include green tea, cocoa powder, the Indian spice turmeric, kale, onions and parsley. Many of the fruit and vegetables on display in supermarkets, such as tomatoes, avocados, bananas, lettuce, kiwis, carrots and cucumber, are actually rather low in sirtuin activators. This doesn't mean that they aren't worth eating, though, as they provide lots of other benefits. The beauty of eating a diet packed with sirtfoods is that it's far more flexible than other diets. You could simply eat healthily adding some sirtfoods on top. Or you could have them in a concentrated way. Adding sirtfoods to say, the 5:2 diet could allow more calories on the low-calorie days.

A remarkable finding of one sirtfood diet trial is that participants lost substantial weight without losing muscle. In fact, it was common for participants to actually gain muscle, leading to a more defined and toned look. That's the beauty of sirtfoods; they activate fat burning but also promote muscle growth, maintenance and repair. This is in complete contrast to other diets where weight loss typically comes from both fat and muscle, with the loss of muscle slowing down metabolism and making weight regain more likely.

GETTING ENOUGH SIRTS

Are you worried that you are not getting enough SIRTs into your diet? Perhaps you have a passionate dislike for kale? Don't worry, there are many different ways to get your daily SIRT requirements. So if there is a food or two you want to avoid, then just steer clear, there are many other options. Have a look through this guide and see what your favourites are.

Think about your green vegetables -ideally one to two portions daily. If you don't like the stronger tasting leafy greens, then perhaps plainer broccoli or cauliflower? You only need a handful of parsley (10g) and it has a mild, unobtrusive taste. You could buy a growing pot of parsley from the supermarket and add a portion to your main meal or a salad. Olive oil and olives – at least one portion a day. Olive oil is such a versatile oil that it can be used in virtually all your cooking. Use extra virgin olive oil in salads and a light and mild version for frying when you don't want an olive oil flavour.getting enough sirts Onions and apples – at least one portion a day. Raw red onion is great in salads or salsa. Many a main dish starts with lightly sauteed onions. And what could be easier than grabbing an apple as a mid-afternoon snack?

Resveratrol: red wine, red grapes, chocolate – at least two portions a day.

Turmeric – at least two portions a week. You only need 1/2 tsp to get a portion of SIRTs from turmeric. Easy to add to Indian and North African dishes.

Oily fish – at least two portions a week. Salmon, trout and mackerel all count. Salmon is especially versatile and is very quick to cook. Or try a nice breakfast of smoked salmon and scrambled eggs. With all these normal everyday foods, it is very easy to increase the amount of SIRTs you eat each day. A few wise decisions will pay huge dividends.

Sirtfood Diet And Exercise

With 52% of Americans confessing that they find it easier to do their taxes than to understand how to eat healthily, it's vital to introduce a form of eating that becomes a way of life rather than a one-off fad diet. For some of us it may not be that difficult to lose weight or retain a healthy weight, but the Sirtfood diet can help those who are struggling. But what about combining the Sirtfood diet with exercise, is it advisable to avoid exercise completely or introduce it once you have started the diet?

The Sirt Diet Principles

With an estimated 650 million obese adults globally, it's important to find healthy eating and exercise regimes that are doable, don't deprive you of everything you enjoy, and don't require you to exercise all week. The Sirtfood diet does just that. The idea is that certain foods will active the 'skinny gene' pathways which are usually activated by fasting and exercise. The good news is that certain food and drink, including dark chocolate and red wine, contain chemicals called polyphenols that activate the genes that mimic the effects of exercise and fasting.

Exercise during the first few weeks

During the first week or two of the diet where your calorie intake is reduced, it would be sensible to stop or reduce exercise while your body adapts to fewer calories. Listen to your body and if you feel fatigued or have less energy than usual, don't work out. Instead ensure that you remain focused on the principles that apply to a healthy lifestyle such as including adequate daily levels of fibre, protein and fruit and vegetables.

Once the diet becomes a way of life

When you do exercise it's important to consume protein ideally an hour after your workout. Protein repairs muscles after exercise, reduces soreness and can aid recovery. There are a variety of recipes which include protein which will be perfect for post-exercise consumption, such as the sirt chilli con carne or the turmeric chicken and kale salad. If you want something lighter you could try the sirt blueberry smoothie and add some protein powder for added benefit. The type of fitness you do will be down to you, but workouts at home will allow you to choose when to exercise, the types of exercises that suit you and are short and convenient.

The Sirtfood diet is great way to change your eating habits, lose weight and feel healthier. The initial few weeks may challenge you but it's important to check which foods are best to eat and which delicious recipes suit you. Be kind to yourself in the first few weeks while your body adapts and take exercise easy if you choose to do it at all. If you are already someone who does moderate or intense exercise then it may be that you can carry on as normal, or manage your fitness in accordance with the change in diet. As with any diet and exercise changes, it's all about the individual and how far you can push yourself.

Spice Up Your Sirtfood Diet With Bird's-Eye Chilies

The Sirtfood Bird's-Eye Chillies contain the major sirtuin-activating nutrients Luteolin and Myricetin.

Bird's-eye chillies(sometimes referred to as 'Thai chillies') are one of the top 20 Sirtfoods and appear regularly in the recipe sections(here and here) of this website. If you are not used to spicy food, it is suggested you start with half the chilli amount stated in the recipe, as well as deseeding your chilli before use. You can adjust the heat to your preference throughout the diet.

Chilli originated in the Americas and has been part of the human diet since at least 7500 BC. Explorer Christopher Columbus brought it back to Spain in the 15th century and its cultivation spread rapidly through the rest of the world. Its pungent heat is designed as a plant defence mechanism to cause discomfort and dissuade predators from feasting on it, yet many relish adding it to their eating patterns.

There are more than 200 varieties, coloured anything from yellow to green to red to black, and varying in heat from mildly warm to mouth-blisteringly hot.

Bird's- Eye Chillies boast much greater sirtuin-activating credentials than the milder standard chillies that are more commonly used. Bird's-Eye chillies are known for weight reducing qualities. They can play a key role in increasing the metabolism of the body by increasing your body temperature. Faster metabolism, proper digestion and waste expulsion, can decrease the chance of fat accumulation in the body. The chemical compound present in Bird's-Eye chilli which results in the burning sensation is called Capsaicin. The effects of this compound can vary among individuals. However, most common is a burning sensation of the mouth, throat, and stomach upon ingestion. It's not just the heat of chillies but the way they enhance the flavours of other ingredients.

Drinking Green Tea

Like it or loathe it drinking green tea is an essential and core part of the SirtFood diet.

If you're already a convert to green tea, then congratulations you'll already be reaping the benefits of the extraordinary sirtuins found in green tea. You'll find weight-loss comes more easily, together with a revitalised spirit and glowing skin.

Green tea is the only source of one of the most powerful sirtuin bioactives, catechin. Catechins are so potent that only a small quantity, one small cup, triggers fat metabolism and reduces oxidative stress.

- Appetite suppressant

With a cup or two of green tea inside you. you really notice the difference in terms of hunger pangs. You should find that you don't think about food between meals.

- A little bit of caffeine

A cup of green tea contains about a quarter of the caffeine you'd find in a cup of coffee or half the caffeine you'd find in a cup of black tea. This caffeine is just enough to combine with the catechins to have an even more powerful fat-burning effect. This is the optimum way to convert fat to muscle.

- More energy

Hard to measure but definitely there, the catechins give you a little natural buzz that makes starting the day a little easier.

- Cumulative effect

The power of green tea keeps on giving and two cups of green tea is better than one cup, three cups is better than two cups. In fact you can get up to four of your SIRT 5 a day from drinking green tea if you have four or more cups.

• Zero calorie

Green tea is naturally calorie free. It doesn't need sugar or sweetener and gives you energy without the calories.

What Are The Best Juicers?

How To Choose The Best Juicers For Making Green Juices

Let's look at the range of juicers available to make the task of preparing your green sirtfood drink as easily as possible.

Types Of Juice Extractors

There are three main types of juicers or juice extractors suitable for your green sirtfood juice. Each type have their own advantages and disadvantages. **Centrifugal Juicers**

Centrifugal juicers are the most freely available of the juicers in retail outlets. They are usually upright and cylindrical in shape. They extract juice from fruits and vegetables by grating them into tiny portions, then using a sieve to extract the juice out of the pulp at high speeds. juicers Advantages: Centrifugal juicers are very fast when making juice so they are very convenient. They usually have larger entry points so you don't have to cut up the greens as much which means less preparation time. They are usually easier to clean than other types of juicers and there is a huge range on the market at all different prices.

Disadvantages: Centrifugal juicers generally do not perform as well when juicing leafy greens. If you are looking at making a better green juice, then look into masticating or triturating juicers. Centrifugal juicers are not as thorough at extracting juice from pulp and they tend to produce foam in the juice. Examples of centrifugal juicers include the Breville Juice Fountain series and the ever popular (and budget-friendly) Jack Lalanne juicer. More information about the range of centrifugal juicer products available can be viewed here.

Masticating Juicers

Masticating or single-gear juicers utilise a screw-type auger to grind, crush and chew fruits, vegetables and leafy greens. It distributes the juice and extracts the pulp into separate containers. Advantages: Masticating juicers do a much better job at juicing leafy greens and vegetables than centrifugal juicers, and produce drier pulp – which means they extract more nutrients. These types of juicers usually last much longer and come with longer warranties. Masticating juicers may also be used to make nut butters, sauces, baby food and pasta as well as fruit sorbet. Disadvantages: Masticating juicers have smaller access points so there is more cutting and chopping of fruits and vegetables when juicing. It takes longer to generate juices with these than it does with a centrifugal juicer. Masticating juicers have more parts and take longer to clean. They are more expensive than centrifugal juicers, although high-end centrifugal juicers are similar in cost to a mid-range masticating juicer. Examples of masticating juicers include the Omega 8005/8006 series and the Champion brand juicers.

More detailed information about different Masticating Juicers can be found right here.

Triturating Juicers

Triturating or twin gear juicers are the most expensive juicers and are considered to be the best on the market. They work in a similar fashion to a masticating juicer but the motor runs slower, which preserves maximum nutrients and promotes efficient juicing. They also have two, interlocking screws that grind, crush and chew produce in order to extract the juice.

Advantages: Triturating juicers are the best you can get. They are the most efficient juicers and extract the maximum amount of juice (and nutrients), which results in the driest pulp (fewer wasted nutrients). As with masticating juicers, triturating juicers can be used to make nut butters, sauces, baby food, pasta and fruit sorbet. Disadvantages: The most expensive. They are not as fast and easy to use and some force is required to push Zulky vegetables into the gripping, twisting gears.

Examples of triturating juicers include the Green Star brand juice extractors. Further information on the range of Triturating Juicers can be obtained from this source.

Juicer Recommendations

Which juicer you should buy depends on how serious you are about juicing.

Tribest Green Star Juicers – Look at one of these juicers if juicing is a serious, daily habit for you. They are the top of the range line of triturating juice extractors and will make the best, most nutrient-rich juice. .

Here is the complete range of the Green Star juicers at Amazon.

Omega 8005/8006 – I own the Omega 8005 masticating juicer and I'm very happy with both the juicer and the juice it makes. I chose the Omega over another popular brand, the Champion, because the Omega is said to do a much better job at juicing leafy greens than the Champion brand. The Omega 8006 is the newest model now replacing the 8005, but the 8005 is less expensive.

Breville 800JEXL Juice Fountain Elite – This centrifugal juicer has a ton of positive reviews on Amazon.com. While I am biased toward masticating juicers because I plan on juicing lots of greens, the Breville 800JEXL claims to handle leafy greens with ease. At just under $300, this juicer is at the same price point as the Omega 8006. However, the Breville will make juices much faster and easier than masticating juicers in the same price range, although the juice may not be extracted as efficiently.

Budget-Friendly Juicer – If you aren't sure whether juicing will become a regular part of your life, then pretty much any juicer will get you started. However, if you plan on juicing with any regularity, or you are serious about the quality of your green juices it is recommended that you spend the extra money on a masticating or triturating juicer. A less expensive juicer might serve your needs now, but you will end up spending more in the long run.

Best Sirtfoods for Good Health

Love red wine and chocolate, but you're trying to slim down? Then you should look at adding more Sirtfoods to your diet. Also referred to as "wonder foods," these products support weight loss and overall health. Their name comes from "sirtuins," a type of protein that regulates biological pathways, metabolism, longevity, and cellular functions. These compounds are known as 'housekeeping genes'.

Sirtfoods are typically high in polyphenols and other antioxidants that activate sirtuins in your body. By including them in your diet, you'll burn more calories and rev up your metabolism. Research indicates that sirtuin activators regulate insulin production, improve mitochondria function, and increase lifespan.

Here are the top 5 foods for Sirt diet

Dark Chocolate :This delicious treat keeps your heart in shape and regulates blood pressure. Rich in antioxidants, dark chocolate delays the aging process and fights free radicals. It also strengthens your body's defense mechanism and wards off diseases. The flavanols in dark chocolate may improve blood flow and reduce oxidative damage.

Green Tea :Loaded with antioxidants and cancer-fighting compounds, green tea is one of the most powerful natural remedies out there. This beverage is made from the dried leaves of the Camellia sinensis plant, which has been shown effective against pancreatic cancer, lung cancer, colorectal cancer, and prostate cancer. Green tea also reduces heart disease risk, lowers bad cholesterol, and protects against stroke. Its weight loss benefits are backed up by science.

Blueberries: Blueberries are an excellent source if vitamin C, vitamin K, manganese, copper, and dietary fiber. They also have the highest antioxidant content of all berries. These popular Sirtfoods boost immunity and neutralize the free radicals that can damage cellular structures. Low in calories and carbs, they're ideal for dieters. Recent studies suggest that blueberries may help reduce stomach fat and risk factors for metabolic syndrome. Rich in calcium, they also strengthen your bones and prevent osteoporosis.

Capers : Capers boast powerful anti-inflammatory effects, offering a cocktail of vitamins, minerals, and antioxidants. They have only 23 calories per 100 grams, and provide large amounts of calcium, potassium, vitamin K, riboflavin, iron, copper, and phytonutrients. Quercentin and rutin, the key antioxidants in capers, have strong analgesic, antibacterial, and anticarcinogenic properties. Rutin helps prevent and treat hemorrhoids, improves circulation, and reduces bad cholesterol levels in obese patients. Quercentin inhibits tumor growth and boosts immune function. The best way to use capers is adding them to salads, pasta, and casseroles.

Turmeric : This spice has been used since ancient times for its healing properties. Curcumin, its active ingredients, is a strong antioxidant and anti-inflammatory agent. This naturally occurring compound reduces inflammation in your body, which helps prevent arthritis, chronic pain, cancer, heart disease, and various degenerative conditions. Turmeric also enhances the body's antioxidant capacity, fights free radial damage, and improves brain function. This is one of the few foods containing BDNF (brain-derived neutrophic factor), a protein that contributes to the growth, maturation, and survival of nerve cells.

These are the 5 best Sirtfoods but there are many other Sirtfoods with proven health benefits, such as apples, kale, citrus fruit, and parsley. Red wine contains sirtuin activators too. Your diet should also include tofu, olive oil, passion fruit, and onions, which stimulate sirtuin genes and boast high antioxidant levels.

New Sirtfood Recipes

Turkey Escalope with sage, caper and parsley and spiced cauliflower 'couscous'-

*150g cauliflower, roughly chopped

*1 clove garlic, finely chopped

*40g red onion, finely chopped

*1 bird's eye chilli, finely chopped

*1tsp fresh ginger, finely chopped

*2tbsp extra virgin olive oil

*2tsp ground turmeric

*30g sun-dried tomatoes, finely chopped

*10g parsley

*150g turkey escalope

*1tsp dried sage

*Juice 1/2 lemon

*1tbsp capers

1 Place the cauliflower in a food processor and pulse in 2-second bursts to finely chop it until it resembles couscous. Set aside. Fry the garlic, red onion, chilli and ginger in 1tsp of the oil until soft but not coloured. Add

the turmeric and cauliflower and cook for 1 minute. Remove from the heat and add the sun-dried tomatoes and half the parsley.

2 Coat the turkey escalope in the remaining oil and sage then fry for 5-6 minutes, turning regularly. When cooked, add the lemon juice, remaining parsley, capers and 1tbsp water to the pan to make a sauce, then serve.

Choc Chip Granola-New Sirtfood Recipesnew sirtfood recipes

244 calories

1/2 of your SIRT 5 a day

Chocolate at breakfast! Be sure to serve with a cup of green tea to give you plenty of SIRTs. The rice malt syrup can be substituted with maple syrup if you prefer.

Serves 8 • Ready in 30 minutes

- 200g jumbo oats
- 50g pecans, roughly chopped
- 3 tbsp light olive oil
- 20g butter
- 1 tbsp dark brown sugar
- 2 tbsp rice malt syrup
- 60g good-quality (70%) dark chocolate chips

1 Preheat the oven to 160°C (140°C fan/Gas 3). Line a large baking tray with a silicone sheet or baking parchment.

2 Mix the oats and pecans together in a large bowl. In a small non-stick pan, gently heat the olive oil, butter, brown sugar and rice malt syrup until the butter has melted and the sugar and syrup have dissolved. Do not allow to boil. Pour the syrup over the oats and stir thoroughly until the oats are fully covered.

3 Distribute the granola over the baking tray, spreading right into the corners. Leave clumps of mixture with spacing rather than an even spread. Bake in the oven for 20 minutes until just tinged golden brown at the edges. Remove from the oven and leave to cool on the tray completely.

4 When cool, break up any bigger lumps on the tray with your fingers and then mix in the chocolate chips. Scoop

or pour the granola into an airtight tub or jar. The granola will keep for at least 2 weeks.

Sirtfood Diet's Braised Puy Lentils-New Sirtfood Recipesnew sirtfood recipes

Serves: 1

Preparation time: 40 – 50 minutes

Ingredients

- 8 Cherry tomatoes, halved
- 2 tsp Extra virgin olive oil
- 40 g Red onion, thinly sliced
- 1 Garlic clove, finely chopped
- 40 g Celery, thinly sliced
- 40 g Carrots, peeled and thinly sliced
- 1 tsp Paprika

- 1 tsp Thyme (dry or fresh)
- 75 g Puy lentils
- 220 ml Vegetable stock
- 50 g Kale, roughly chopped
- 1 tbsp Parsley, chopped
- 20 g Rocket

Method

1. Heat your oven to 120ºC/gas ½.

2. Put the tomatoes into a small roasting tin and roast in the oven for 35–45 minutes.

3. Heat a saucepan over a low–medium heat. Add 1 teaspoon of the olive oil with the red onion, garlic, celery and carrot and fry for 1–2 minutes, until softened. Stir in the paprika and thyme and cook for a further minute.

4. Rinse the lentils in a fine-meshed sieve and add them to the pan along with the stock. Bring to the boil, then

reduce the heat and simmer gently for 20 minutes with a lid on the pan. Give the pan a stir every 7 minutes or so, adding a little water if the level drops too much.

5. Add the kale and cook for a further 10 minutes. When the lentils are cooked, stir in the parsley and roasted tomatoes. Serve with the rocket drizzled with the remaining teaspoon of olive oil.

Sirtfood Diet's Shakshuka-New Sirtfood Recipesnew sirtfood recipes

Enjoy this healthy recipe of spicy baked eggs and kale

Serves: 1

Preparation time: 40 minutes

Ingredients

- 1 tsp Extra virgin olive oil
- 40g Red onion, finely chopped
- 1 Garlic clove, finely chopped
- 30g Celery, finely chopped
- 1 Bird's eye chilli, finely chopped
- 1 tsp Ground cumin
- 1 tsp Ground turmeric
- 1 tsp Paprika
- 400g Tinned chopped tomatoes
- 30g Kale, stems removed and roughly chopped
- 1 tbsp Chopped parsley
- 2 Medium eggs

Method

1. Heat a small, deep-sided frying pan over a medium–low heat. Add the oil and fry the onion, garlic, celery, chilli and spices for 1–2 minutes.

2. Add the tomatoes, then leave the sauce to simmer gently for 20 minutes, stirring occasionally.

3. Add the kale and cook for a further 5 minutes. If you feel the sauce is getting too thick, simply add a little water. When your sauce has a nice rich consistency, stir in the parsley.

4. Make two little wells in the sauce and crack each egg into them. Reduce the heat to its lowest setting and cover the pan with a lid or foil. Leave the eggs to cook for 10–12 minutes, at which point the whites should be firm while the yolks are still runny. Cook for a further 3–4 minutes if you prefer the yolks to be firm. Serve immediately – ideally straight from the pan.

Vietnamese Turmeric Fish with Herbs & Mango Sauce- New Sirtfood Recipes

Prep time: 15 mins Cook time 30 mins Total 45 minutes

Serves 4new sirtfood receipes

Ingredients

Fish:

* 1 ¼ lbs fresh cod fish, boneless and skinless, cut into 2-inch piece wide that are about ½ inch thick

* 2 tbsp coconut oil to pan-fry the fish (plus a few more tablespoon if necessary)

* Small pinch of sea salt to taste

Fish marinade: (Marinate for at least 1 hr. or as long as overnight)

* 1 tbsp turmeric powder

* 1 tsp sea salt

* 1 tbsp Chinese cooking wine (Alt. dry sherry)

* 2 tsp minced ginger

* 2 tbsp olive oil

Infused Scallion and Dill Oil:

* 2 cups scallions (slice into long thin shape)

* 2 cups of fresh dill

* Pinch of sea salt to taste.

Mango dipping sauce:

* 1 medium sized ripe mango

* 2 tbsp rice vinegar

* Juice of ½ lime

1 garlic clove

1 tsp dry red chili pepper (stir in before serving)

Toppings:

* Fresh cilantro (as much as you like)

* Lime juice (as much as you like)

* Nuts (cashew or pine nuts)

Instructions

Steps:

1. Marinate the fish for at least 1 hr. or as long as overnight.

2. Place all ingredients under "Mango Dipping Sauce" into a food processor and blend until desired consistency.

To Pan-Fry The Fish:

1. Heat 2 tbsp of coconut oil in a non-stick large frying pan over high heat. When hot, add the pre-marinated fish. *Note: place the fish slices into the pan individually and separate to two or more batches to pan fry if necessary.

2. You should hear a loud sizzle, after which you can decrease the heat to medium-high.

3. Do not turn or move the fish until you see a golden brown color on the side, about 5 minutes. Season with a pinch of sea salt. Add more coconut oil to pan-fry the fish if necessary.

4. Once the fish is in golden brown color carefully turn the fish to fry on the other side. Once it's done, transfer to a large plate. *Note: There should be some oil left in the frying pan. We use the remainder of the oil to make scallion and dill infused oil.

To Make The Scallion And Dill Infused Oil:

1. Use the remainder of the oil in the frying pan over medium-high heat, add 2 cups of scallions and 2 cups of dill. Turn off the heat once you have added the scallions and dill. Give them a gentle toss just until the scallions and dill have wilted, about 15 seconds. Season with a dash of sea salt.

2. Pour the scallion, dill, and infused oil over the fish and serve with mango dipping sauce with fresh cilantro, lime, and nuts.

Moroccan Spiced Eggs-New Sirtfood Recipes

394 calories

SERVES 2 • READY IN 50 MINUTES

new sirtfood recipes

- 1 tsp olive oil

- 1 shallot, peeled and finely chopped
- 1 red (bell) pepper, deseeded and finely chopped
- 1 garlic clove, peeled and finely chopped
- 1 courgette (zucchini), peeled and finely chopped
- 1 tbsp tomato puree (paste)
- ½ tsp mild chilli powder
- ¼ tsp ground cinnamon
- ¼ tsp ground cumin
- ½ tsp salt
- 1 × 400g (14oz) can chopped tomatoes
- 1 x 400g (14oz) can chickpeas in water
- small handful of flat-leaf parsley (10g (1/3oz)), chopped
- 4 medium eggs at room temperature

• Heat the oil in a saucepan, add the shallot and red (bell) pepper and fry gently for 5 minutes. Then add the garlic and courgette (zucchini) and cook for another minute or two. Add the tomato puree (paste), spices and salt and stir through.

• Add the chopped tomatoes and chickpeas (soaking liquor and all) and increase the heat to medium. With the lid off the pan, simmer the sauce for 30 minutes – make sure it is gently bubbling throughout and allow it to reduce in volume by about one-third.

• Remove from the heat and stir in the chopped parsley.

• Preheat the oven to 200C/180C fan/350F.

• When you are ready to cook the eggs, bring the tomato sauce up to a gentle simmer and transfer to a small oven-proof dish.

• Crack the eggs on the side of the dish and lower them gently into the stew. Cover with foil and bake in the oven for 10-15 minutes. Serve the concoction in individual bowls with the eggs floating on the top.

Raw Brownie Bites-New Sirtfood Recipes

new sirtfood recipes

Total Time: 5 minutes

Serves: 6

INGREDIENTS:

- 2½ cups whole walnuts
- ¼ cup almonds
- 2½ cups Medjool dates
- 1 cup cacao powder
- 1 teaspoon vanilla extract
- ⅛-¼ teaspoon sea salt

DIRECTIONS:

Place everything in a food processor until well combined.

Roll into balls and place on a baking sheet and freeze for 30 minutes or refrigerate for 2 hours.

Waldorf Salad -New Sirtfood Recipes

Ingredients (serves 2)

- 200g celery, roughly chopped

- 100g apple, roughly chopped

- 50g walnuts, roughly chopped

- 1 small red onion, roughly chopped

- 1 head of chicory, chopped

- 10g flat parsley, chopped

- 1 tbsp capers

- 10g lovage or celery leaves, roughly chopped

- For the dressing:

- 1 tbsp extra virgin olive oil

- 1 tsp balsamic vinegar

- 1 teaspoon Dijon mustard

- Juice of half a lemon

Mix the celery, apple, walnuts, onion, parsley, capers and lovage/celery in a medium-sized salad bowl and mix. Make the dressing by whisking together the oil, vinegar, mustard and lemon juice. Drizzle over the salad, mix and serve!

Chargrilled Beef With A Red Wine Jus, Onion Rings, Garlic, Kale And Herb Roasted Potatoes-New Sirtfood Recipes

INGREDIENTS:

- 100g potatoes, peeled and cut into 2cm dice
- 1 tbsp extra virgin olive oil
- 5g parsley, finely chopped
- 50g red onion, sliced into rings
- 50g kale, sliced
- 1 garlic clove, finely chopped
- 120–150g x 3.5cm-thick beef fillet steak or 2cm-thick sirloin steak
- 40ml red wine
- 150ml beef stock
- 1 tsp tomato purée
- 1 tsp cornflour, dissolved in 1 tbsp water

INSTRUCTIONS:

Heat the oven to 220ºC/gas 7.

Place the potatoes in a saucepan of boiling water, bring back to the boil and cook for 4–5 minutes, then drain. Place in a roasting tin with 1 teaspoon of the oil and roast in the hot oven for 35–45 minutes. Turn the potatoes every 10 minutes to ensure even cooking. When cooked, remove from the oven, sprinkle with the chopped parsley and mix well.

Fry the onion in 1 teaspoon of the oil over a medium heat for 5–7 minutes, until soft and nicely caramelised. Keep warm. Steam the kale for 2–3 minutes then drain. Fry the garlic gently in ½ teaspoon of oil for 1 minute, until soft but not coloured. Add the kale and fry for a further 1–2 minutes, until tender. Keep warm.

Heat an ovenproof frying pan over a high heat until smoking. Coat the meat in ½ a teaspoon of the oil and fry in the hot pan over a medium–high heat according to how you like your meat done. If you like your meat medium it would be better to sear the meat and then transfer the pan to an oven set at 220ºC/gas 7 and finish the cooking that way for the prescribed times. Remove the meat from the pan and set aside to rest. Add the wine to the hot pan to bring up any meat residue. Bubble to reduce the wine by half, until syrupy and with a concentrated flavor.

Add the stock and tomato purée to the steak pan and bring to the boil, then add the cornflour paste to thicken your sauce, adding it a little at a time until you have your desired consistency. Stir in any of the juices from the rested steak and serve with the roasted potatoes, kale, onion rings and red wine sauce.

Fresh Saag Paneer-New Sirtfood Recipes

- 279 calories
- 3 of your SIRT 5 a day

Serves 2 • Ready in 20 minutes

- 2 tsp rapeseed oil
- 200g paneer. cut into cubes
- Salt and freshly ground black pepper
- 1 red onion, chopped
- 1 small thumb (3 cm) fresh ginger, peeled and cut into matchsticks
- 1 clove garlic, peeled and thinly sliced

- 1 green chilli, deseeded and finely sliced
- 100g cherry tomatoes, halved
- 1/2 tsp ground coriander
- 1/2 tsp ground cumin
- 1/4 tsp ground turmeric
- 1/2 tsp mild chilli powder
- 1/2 tsp salt
- 100g fresh spinach leaves
- Small handful (10g) parsley, chopped
- Small handful (10g) coriander, chopped

1 Heat the oil in a wide lidded frying pan over a high heat. Season the paneer generously with salt and pepper and toss into the pan. Fry for a few minutes until golden, stirring often. Remove from the pan with a slotted spoon and set aside.

2 Reduce the heat and add the onion. Fry for 5 minutes before adding the ginger, garlic and chilli. Cook for another couple of minutes before adding the cherry tomatoes. Put the lid on the pan and cook for a further 5 minutes.

3 Add the spices and salt, then stir. Return the paneer to the pan and stir until coated. Add the spinach to the pan together with the parsley and coriander and put the lid on. Allow the spinach to wilt for 1-2 minutes, then incorporate into the dish. Serve immediately.

Mocha Chocolate Mousse-New Sirtfood Recipes

new sirtfood recipes

Everyone enjoys chocolate mousse and this one has a wonderful light and airy texture. It is quick and easy to make and is best served the day after it's made.

Serves 4–6

Ingredients

- 250g dark chocolate (85% cocoa solids)
- 6 medium free-range eggs, separated
- 4 tbsp strong black coffee
- 4 tbsp almond milk
- Chocolate coffee beans, to decorate

Method:

1. Melt the chocolate in a large bowl set over a pan of gently simmering water, making sure the bottom of the

bowl doesn't touch the water. Remove the bowl from the heat and leave the melted chocolate to cool to room temperature.

2. Once the melted chocolate is at room temperature, whisk in the egg yolks one at a time and then gently fold in the coffee and almond milk.

3. Using a hand-held electric mixer, whisk the egg whites until stiff peaks form, then mix a couple of tablespoons into the chocolate mixture to loosen it. Gently fold in the remainder, using a large metal spoon.

4. Transfer the mousse to individual glasses and smooth the surface. Cover with cling film and chill for at least 2 hours, ideally overnight. Decorate with chocolate coffee beans before serving.

Buckwheat Superfood Muesli - New Sirtfood Recipes

new sirtfood recipes

INGREDIENTS

- 20g buckwheat flakes
- 10g buckwheat puffs
- 15g coconut flakes or desiccated coconut
- 40g Medjool dates, pitted and chopped
- 15g walnuts, chopped
- 10g cocoa nibs
- 100g strawberries, hulled and chopped
- 100g plain Greek yogurt (or vegan alternative, such as soy or coconut yogurt)

INSTRUCTIONS

Mix all of the above ingredients together (leave out the strawberries and yogurt if not serving straight away).

NOTES

If you want to make this in bulk or prepare it the night before, simply combine the dry ingredients and store it in an airtight container. All you need to do the next day is add the strawberries and yogurt and it's good to go.

Buckwheat Pancakes With Strawberries, Dark Chocolate Sauce And Crushed Walnuts-New Sirtfood Recipes

Makes around 6 to 8 pancakes, depending on the size. recipes sirtfood

For the pancakes you will need:

- 350ml milk
- 150g buckwheat flour
- 1 large egg
- 1 tbsp extra virgin olive oil, for cooking
- For the chocolate sauce
- 100g dark chocolate (85 percent cocoa solids)
- 85ml milk
- 1 tbsp double cream
- 1 tbsp extra virgin olive oil

To serve

- 400g strawberries, hulled and chopped
- 100g walnuts, chopped

To make the pancake batter, place all of the ingredients apart from the olive oil in a blender and blend until you have a smooth batter. It should not be too thick or too runny. (You can store any excess batter in an airtight container for up to 5 days in your fridge. Be sure to mix well before using again.)

To make the chocolate sauce, melt the chocolate in a heatproof bowl over a pan of simmering water. Once melted, mix in the milk, whisking thoroughly and then add the double cream and olive oil. You can keep the sauce warm by leaving the water in the pan simmering on a very low heat until your pancakes are ready. To make the pancakes heat a heavy-bottomed frying pan until it starts to smoke, then add the olive oil.

Pour some of the batter into the centre of the pan, then tip the excess batter around it until you have covered the whole surface, you may have to add a little more batter to achieve this. You will only need to cook the pancake for 1 minute or so on each side if your pan is hot enough.

Once you can see it going brown around the edges use a spatula to loosen the pancake around its edge, then flip it over. Try to flip in one action to avoid breaking it. Cook for a further minute or so on the other side and transfer to a plate. Place some strawberries in the centre and roll up the pancake. Continue until you have made as many pancakes as required. Spoon over a generous amount of sauce and sprinkle over some chopped walnuts.

You may find that your first efforts are too fat or fall apart but once you find the consistency of your batter that works best for you and you get your technique perfected you'll be making them like a professional. Practice makes perfect in this case.

Blueberry Banana Pancakes with Chunky Apple Compote and Golden Tumeric Latte-New Sirtfood Recipes

Ingredients

For the Blueberry Banana Pancakes

- 6 bananas
- 6 eggs
- 150g rolled oats
- 2 tsp baking powder
- ¼ teaspoon salt
- 25g blueberries

- 2 apples
- 5 dates (pitted)
- 1 tablespoon lemon juice
- 1/4 teaspoon cinnamon powder
- pinch salt

- 3 cups coconut milk
- 1 teaspoon turmeric powder
- 1 teaspoon cinnamon powder
- 1 teaspoon raw honey
- Pinch of black pepper (increases absorption)
- Tiny piece of fresh, peeled ginger root
- Pinch of cayenne pepper (optional)

Instructions

For the Blueberry Banana Pancakes

1. Pop the rolled oats in a high-speed blender and pulse for 1 minute or until an oat flour has formed. Tip: make sure your blender is very dry before doing this or else everything will become soggy!

2.Now add the bananas, eggs, baking powder and salt to the blender and pulse for 2 minutes until a smooth batter forms.

3.Transfer the mixture to a large bowl and fold in the blueberries. Leave to rest for 10 mins whilst the baking powder activates.

4.To make your pancakes, add a dollop of butter (this helps to make them really delicious and crispy!) to your frying pan on a medium-high heat. Add a few spoons of the blueberry pancake mix and fry for until nicely golden on the bottom side. Toss the pancake to fry the other side.

For the Chunky Apple Compote

1.Core and rough chop your apples.

2.Pop everything in a food processor, together with 2 tablespoons of water and a pinch of salt. Pulse to form your chunky apple compote.

For the Golden Turmeric Latte

1.Blend all ingredients in a high-speed blender until smooth.

2.Pour into a small pan and heat for 4 minutes over medium heat until hot but not boiling.

3.Enjoy!

Blueberry Smoothie-New Sirtfood Recipes   new sirtfood recipes

160 calories

1 of your SIRT 5 a day

This yogurt smoothie has a rich, creamy taste.

Serves 2 • Ready in 2 minutes

- 1 ripe banana
- 100g blueberries
- 100g blackberries
- 2 tbsp natural yogurt
- 200ml milk

Blend all the ingredients together until smooth.

Savory Turmeric Pancakes With Lemon Yogurt Sauce- New Sirtfood Recipes

new sirtfood recipes

Serves: 8 pancakes

Ingredients

For The Yogurt Sauce

- 1 cup plain Greek yogurt
- 1 garlic clove, minced
- 1 to 2 tablespoons lemon juice (from 1 lemon), to taste
- ¼ teaspoon ground turmeric
- 10 fresh mint leaves, minced
- 2 teaspoons lemon zest (from 1 lemon)

- For The Pancakes
- 2 teaspoons ground turmeric
- 1½ teaspoons ground cumin
- 1 teaspoon salt
- 1 teaspoon ground coriander
- ½ teaspoon garlic powder
- ½ teaspoon freshly ground black pepper
- 1 head broccoli, cut into florets
- 3 large eggs, lightly beaten
- 2 tablespoons plain unsweetened almond milk
- 1 cup almond flour
- 4 teaspoons coconut oil

Instructions

1.Make the yogurt sauce. Combine the yogurt, garlic, lemon juice, turmeric, mint and zest in a bowl. Taste and season with more lemon juice, if needed. Set aside or refrigerate until ready to serve.

2.Make the pancakes. In a small bowl, combine the turmeric, cumin, salt, coriander, garlic and pepper.

3.Place the broccoli in a food processor, and pulse until the florets are broken up into small pieces. Transfer the broccoli to a large bowl and add the eggs, almond milk, and almond flour. Stir in the spice mix and combine well.

4.Heat 1 teaspoon of the coconut oil in a nonstick pan over medium-low heat. Pour ¼ cup batter into the skillet. Cook the pancake until small bubbles begin to appear on the surface and the bottom is golden brown, 2 to 3 minutes. Flip over and cook the pancake for 2 to 3 minutes more. To keep warm, transfer the cooked pancakes to an oven-safe dish and place in a 200°F oven.

5.Continue making the remaining 3 pancakes, using the remaining oil and batter.

Sirt Chilli Con Carne-New Sirtfood Recipes new sirtfood recipes

Serves 4

- 1 red onion, finely chopped
- 3 garlic cloves, finely chopped
- 2 bird's eye chillies, finely chopped
- 1 tbsp extra virgin olive oil
- 1 tbsp ground cumin
- 1 tbsp ground turmeric
- 400g lean minced beef (5 per cent fat)
- 150ml red wine
- 1 red pepper, cored, seeds removed and cut into bite-sized pieces
- 2 x 400g tins chopped tomatoes
- 1 tbsp tomato purée
- 1 tbsp cocoa powder

- 150g tinned kidney beans
- 300ml beef stock
- 5g coriander, chopped
- 5g parsley, chopped
- 160g buckwheat

In a casserole, fry the onion, garlic and chilli in the oil over a medium heat for 2-3 minutes, then add the spices and cook for a minute. Add the minced beef and brown over a high heat. Add the red wine and allow it to bubble to reduce it by half. Add the red pepper, tomatoes, tomato purée, cocoa, kidney beans and stock and leave to simmer for 1 hour. You may have to add a little water to achieve a thick, sticky consistency. Just before serving, stir in the chopped herbs. Meanwhile, cook the buckwheat according to the packet instructions and serve with the chilli. Chickpea, Quinoa and Turmeric Curry Recipe-New Sirtfood Recipesnew sirtfood recipes

Serves 6

Ingredients

- 500g new potatoes, halved
- 3 garlic cloves, crushed
- 3 teaspoons ground turmeric
- 1 teaspoon ground coriander
- 1 teaspoon chilli flakes or powder
- 1 teaspoon ground ginger
- 400g can of coconut milk
- 1 tbsp tomato purée
- 400g can of chopped tomatoes
- salt and pepper
- 180g quinoa
- 400g can of chickpeas, drained and rinsed
- 150g spinach

Method

Place the potatoes in a pan of cold water and bring to the boil, then let them cook for about 25 minutes until you can easily stick a knife through them. Drain them well.

Place the potatoes in a large pan and add the garlic, turmeric, coriander, chilli, ginger, coconut milk, tomato purée and tomatoes. Bring to the boil, season with salt and pepper, then add the quinoa with a mug of just-boiled water (300ml).

Reduce the heat to a simmer, place the lid on and allow to cook. Over the next 30 minutes, stirring every 5 minutes or so to make sure nothing sticks to the bottom. (This is quite a long cooking time, but this is how long quinoa takes to cook in all these ingredients, rather than just in water.) Halfway through cooking, add the chickpeas. When there are just 5 minutes left, add the spinach and stir it in until it wilts. Once the quinoa has cooked and is fluffy, not crunchy, it's ready. If you like a bit of heat, add a sliced red chilli to the cooking curry at the same time as the other spices.

The Best Sirtfood Recipes

TURMERIC CHICKEN & KALE SALAD WITH HONEY LIME DRESSING-SIRTFOOD RECIPES

Prep time sirtfood recipes

20 mins

Cook time

10 mins

Total time

30 mins

Notes: If preparing ahead of time, dress the salad 10 minutes before serving. Chicken can be replaced with beef mince, chopped prawns or fish. Vegetarians could use chopped mushrooms or cooked quinoa.

Serves: 2

Ingredients

For the chicken

* 1 teaspoon ghee or 1 tbsp coconut oil

* ½ medium brown onion, diced

* 250-300 g / 9 oz. chicken mince or diced up chicken thighs

* 1 large garlic clove, finely diced

* 1 teaspoon turmeric powder

* 1teaspoon lime zest

* juice of ½ lime

* ½ teaspoon salt + pepper

For the salad

* 6 broccolini stalks or 2 cups of broccoli florets

* 2 tablespoons pumpkin seeds (pepitas)

* 3 large kale leaves, stems removed and chopped

* ½ avocado, sliced

* handful of fresh coriander leaves, chopped

* handful of fresh parsley leaves, chopped

For the dressing

* 3 tablespoons lime juice

* 1 small garlic clove, finely diced or grated

* 3 tablespoons extra-virgin olive oil (I used 1 tablespoons avocado oil and * 2 tablespoons EVO)

*1 teaspoon raw honey

* ½ teaspoon wholegrain or Dijon mustard

* ½ teaspoon sea salt and pepper

Instructions

1. Heat the ghee or coconut oil in a small frying pan over medium-high heat. Add the onion and sauté on medium heat for 4-5 minutes, until golden. Add the chicken mince

and garlic and stir for 2-3 minutes over medium-high heat, breaking it apart.

2. Add the turmeric, lime zest, lime juice, salt and pepper and cook, stirring frequently, for a further 3-4 minutes. Set the cooked mince aside.

3. While the chicken is cooking, bring a small saucepan of water to boil. Add the broccolini and cook for 2 minutes. Rinse under cold water and cut into 3-4 pieces each.

4. Add the pumpkin seeds to the frying pan from the chicken and toast over medium heat for 2 minutes, stirring frequently to prevent burning. Season with a little salt. Set aside. Raw pumpkin seeds are also fine to use.

5. Place chopped kale in a salad bowl and pour over the dressing. Using your hands, toss and massage the kale with the dressing. This will soften the kale, kind of like

what citrus juice does to fish or beef carpaccio – it 'cooks' it slightly.

6. Finally toss through the cooked chicken, broccolini, fresh herbs, pumpkin seeds and avocado slices.

BUCKWHEAT NOODLES WITH CHICKEN KALE & MISO DRESSING-SIRTFOOD RECIPESsirtfood recipes

Prep time: 15 mins Cook time: 15 mins Total time: 30 mins

Serves: 2

Ingredients

For the noodles

* 2-3 handfuls of kale leaves (removed from the stem and roughly cut)

* 150 g / 5 oz buckwheat noodles (100% buckwheat, no wheat)

* 3-4 shiitake mushrooms, sliced

* 1 teaspoon coconut oil or ghee

* 1 brown onion, finely diced

* 1 medium free-range chicken breast, sliced or diced

* 1 long red chilli, thinly sliced (seeds in or out depending on how hot you like it)

* 2 large garlic cloves, finely diced

* 2-3 tablespoons Tamari sauce (gluten-free soy sauce)

For the miso dressing

* 1½ tablespoon fresh organic miso

* 1 tablespoon Tamari sauce

* 1 tablespoon extra-virgin olive oil

* 1 tablespoon lemon or lime juice

* 1 teaspoon sesame oil (optional)

Instructions

1. Bring a medium saucepan of water to boil. Add the kale and cook for 1 minute, until slightly wilted. Remove and set aside but reserve the water and bring it back to the boil. Add the soba noodles and cook according to the package instructions (usually about 5 minutes). Rinse under cold water and set aside.

2. In the meantime, pan fry the shiitake mushrooms in a little ghee or coconut oil (about a teaspoon) for 2-3 minutes, until lightly browned on each side. Sprinkle with sea salt and set aside.

3. In the same frying pan, heat more coconut oil or ghee over medium-high heat. Sauté onion and chilli for 2-3

minutes and then add the chicken pieces. Cook 5 minutes over medium heat, stirring a couple of times, then add the garlic, tamari sauce and a little splash of water. Cook for a further 2-3 minutes, stirring frequently until chicken is cooked through.

4. Finally, add the kale and soba noodles and toss through the chicken to warm up.

5. Mix the miso dressing and drizzle over the noodles right at the end of cooking, this way you will keep all those beneficial probiotics in the miso alive and active.

ASIAN KING PRAWN STIR-FRY WITH BUCKWHEAT NOODLES —SIRTFOOD RECIPESsirtfood recipes

Serves 1

Ingredients:

- 150g shelled raw king prawns, deveined
- 2 tsp tamari (you can use soy sauce if you are not avoiding gluten)
- 2 tsp extra virgin olive oil
- 75g soba (buckwheat noodles)
- 1 garlic clove, finely chopped
- 1 bird's eye chilli, finely chopped
- 1 tsp finely chopped fresh ginger
- 20g red onions, sliced
- 40g celery, trimmed and sliced
- 75g green beans, chopped
- 50g kale, roughly chopped
- 100ml chicken stock
- 5g lovage or celery leaves

Instructions:

Heat a frying pan over a high heat, then cook the prawns in 1 teaspoon of the tamari and 1 teaspoon of the oil for 2–3 minutes. Transfer the prawns to a plate. Wipe the pan out with kitchen paper, as you're going to use it again.

Cook the noodles in boiling water for 5–8 minutes or as directed on the packet. Drain and set aside.

Meanwhile, fry the garlic, chilli and ginger, red onion, celery, beans and kale in the remaining oil over a medium–high heat for 2–3 minutes. Add the stock and bring to the boil, then simmer for a minute or two, until the vegetables are cooked but still crunchy.

Add the prawns, noodles and lovage/celery leaves to the pan, bring back to the boil then remove from the heat and serve.

BAKED SALMON SALAD WITH CREAMY MINT DRESSING- SIRTFOOD RECIPESsirtfood recipes

340 calories • 3 of your SIRT 5 a day

Baking the salmon in the oven makes this salad so simple.

Serves 1 • Ready in 20 minutes

- 1 salmon fillet (130g)
- 40g mixed salad leaves
- 40g young spinach leaves
- 2 radishes, trimmed and thinly sliced
- 5cm piece (50g) cucumber, cut into chunks
- 2 spring onions, trimmed and sliced
- 1 small handful (10g) parsley, roughly chopped

For the dressing:

- 1 tsp low-fat mayonnaise
- 1 tbsp natural yogurt
- 1 tbsp rice vinegar
- 2 leaves mint, finely chopped
- Salt and freshly ground black pepper

1 Preheat the oven to 200°C (180°C fan/Gas 6).

2 Place the salmon fillet on a baking tray and bake for 16–18 minutes until just cooked through. Remove from the oven and set aside. The salmon is equally nice hot or cold in the salad. If your salmon has skin, simply cook skin side down and remove the salmon from the skin using a fish slice after cooking. It should slide off easily when cooked.

3 In a small bowl, mix together the mayonnaise, yogurt, rice wine vinegar, mint leaves and salt and pepper

together and leave to stand for at least 5 minutes to allow the flavors to develop.

4 Arrange the salad leaves and spinach on a serving plate and top with the radishes, cucumber, spring onions and parsley. Flake the cooked salmon onto the salad and drizzle the dressing over.

sirtfood recipesCHOC CHIP GRANOLA-SIRTFOOD RECIPES

- 244 calories
- 1/2 of your SIRT 5 a day

Chocolate at breakfast! Be sure to serve with a cup of green tea to give you plenty of SIRTs. The rice malt syrup can be substituted with maple syrup if you prefer.

Serves 8 • Ready in 30 minutes

- 200g jumbo oats
- 50g pecans, roughly chopped
- 3 tbsp light olive oil
- 20g butter
- 1 tbsp dark brown sugar
- 2 tbsp rice malt syrup
- 60g good-quality (70%) dark chocolate chips

1 Preheat the oven to 160°C (140°C fan/Gas 3). Line a large baking tray with a silicone sheet or baking parchment.

2 Mix the oats and pecans together in a large bowl. In a small non-stick pan, gently heat the olive oil, butter, brown sugar and rice malt syrup until the butter has melted and the sugar and syrup have dissolved. Do not allow to boil. Pour the syrup over the oats and stir thoroughly until the oats are fully covered.

3 Distribute the granola over the baking tray, spreading right into the corners. Leave clumps of mixture with spacing rather than an even spread. Bake in the oven for 20 minutes until just tinged golden brown at the edges. Remove from the oven and leave to cool on the tray completely.

4 When cool, break up any bigger lumps on the tray with your fingers and then mix in the chocolate chips. Scoop

or pour the granola into an airtight tub or jar. The granola will keep for at least 2 weeks. FRAGRANT ASIAN HOTPOT- SIRTFOOD RECIPES   sirtfood recipes

185 calories

1 1/2 of you SIRT 5 a day

Serves 2 • Ready in 15 minutes

- 1 tsp tomato purée
- 1 star anise, crushed (or 1/4 tsp ground anise)
- Small handful (10g) parsley, stalks finely chopped
- Small handful (10g) coriander, stalks finely chopped
- Juice of 1/2 lime
- 500ml chicken stock, fresh or made with 1 cube
- 1/2 carrot, peeled and cut into matchsticks

- 50g broccoli, cut into small florets
- 50g beansprouts
- 100g raw tiger prawns
- 100g firm tofu, chopped
- 50g rice noodles, cooked according to packet instructions
- 50g cooked water chestnuts, drained
- 20g sushi ginger, chopped
- 1 tbsp good-quality miso paste

Place the tomato purée, star anise, parsley stalks, coriander stalks, lime juice and chicken stock in a large pan and bring to a simmer for 10 minutes. Add the carrot, broccoli, prawns, tofu, noodles and water chestnuts and simmer gently until the prawns are cooked through. Remove from the heat and stir in the sushi ginger and miso paste. Serve sprinkled with the parsley and coriander leaves.

LAMB, BUTTERNUT SQUASH AND DATE TAGINE- SIRTFOOD RECIPES

Prep timesirtfood recipes

15 mins

Cook time

1 hour 15 mins

Total time

1 hour 30 mins

Incredible warming Moroccan spices make this healthy tagine perfect for chilly autumn and winter evenings. Serve with buckwheat for an extra health kick!

Serves: 4

Ingredients

- 2 tablespoons olive oil
- 1 red onion, sliced
- 2cm ginger, grated
- 3 garlic cloves, grated or crushed
- 1 teaspoon chilli flakes (or to taste)
- 2 teaspoons cumin seeds
- 1 cinnamon stick
- 2 teaspoons ground turmeric
- 800g lamb neck fillet, cut into 2cm chunks
- ½ teaspoon salt
- 100g medjool dates, pitted and chopped

- 400g tin chopped tomatoes, plus half a can of water
- 500g butternut squash, chopped into 1cm cubes
- 400g tin chickpeas, drained
- 2 tablespoons fresh coriander (plus extra for garnish)
- Buckwheat, couscous, flatbreads or rice to serve

Method

1. Preheat your oven to 140C.

2. Drizzle about 2 tablespoons of olive oil into a large ovenproof saucepan or cast iron casserole dish. Add the sliced onion and cook on a gentle heat, with the lid on, for about 5 minutes, until the onions are softened but not brown.

3. Add the grated garlic and ginger, chilli, cumin, cinnamon and turmeric. Stir well and cook for 1 more minute with the lid off. Add a splash of water if it gets too dry.

4. Next add in the lamb chunks. Stir well to coat the meat in the onions and spices and then add the salt, chopped dates and tomatoes, plus about half a can of water (100-200ml).

5. Bring the tagine to the boil and then put the lid on and put in your preheated oven for 1 hour and 15 minutes.

6. Thirty minutes before the end of the cooking time, add in the chopped butternut squash and drained chickpeas. Stir everything together, put the lid back on and return to the oven for the final 30 minutes of cooking.

7.When the tagine is ready, remove from the oven and stir through the chopped coriander. Serve with buckwheat, couscous, flatbreads or basmati rice.

Notes

If you don't own an ovenproof saucepan or cast iron casserole dish, simply cook the tagine in a regular saucepan up until it has to go in the oven and then transfer the tagine into a regular lidded casserole dish before placing in the oven. Add on an extra 5 minutes cooking time to allow for the fact that the casserole dish will need extra time to heat up.

PRAWN ARRABBIATA-SIRTFOOD RECIPES

sirtfood recipes

Serves 1

Preparation time:

35 – 40 minutes

Cooking time:

20 – 30 minutes

Ingredients

- 125-150 g Raw or cooked prawns (Ideally king prawns)
- 65 g Buckwheat pasta
- 1 tbsp Extra virgin olive oil
- For arrabbiata sauce
- 40 g Red onion, finely chopped
- 1 Garlic clove, finely chopped
- 30 g Celery, finely chopped
- 1 Bird's eye chilli, finely chopped

- 1 tsp Dried mixed herbs
- 1 tsp Extra virgin olive oil
- 2 tbsp White wine (optional)
- 400 g Tinned chopped tomatoes
- 1 tbsp Chopped parsley

Method

1. Fry the onion, garlic, celery and chilli and dried herbs in the oil over a medium–low heat for 1–2 minutes. Turn the heat up to medium, add the wine and cook for 1 minute. Add the tomatoes and leave the sauce to simmer over a medium–low heat for 20–30 minutes, until it has a nice rich consistency. If you feel the sauce is getting too thick simply add a little water.

2. While the sauce is cooking bring a pan of water to the boil and cook the pasta according to the packet

instructions. When cooked to your liking, drain, toss with the olive oil and keep in the pan until needed.

3. If you are using raw prawns add them to the sauce and cook for a further 3–4 minutes, until they have turned pink and opaque, add the parsley and serve. If you are using cooked prawns add them with the parsley, bring the sauce to the boil and serve.

4. Add the cooked pasta to the sauce, mix thoroughly but gently and serve.

TURMERIC BAKED SALMON-SIRTFOOD RECIPESsirtfood recipes

Serves: 1

Preparation time:

10 – 15 minutes

Cooking time:

10 minutes

Ingredients

- 125-150 g Skinned Salmon
- 1 tsp Extra virgin olive oil
- 1 tsp Ground turmeric
- 1/4 Juice of a lemon
- For the spicy celery
- 1 tsp Extra virgin olive oil
- 40 g Red onion, finely chopped
- 60 g Tinned green lentils
- 1 Garlic clove, finely chopped
- 1 cm Fresh ginger, finely chopped
- 1 Bire's eye chilli, finely chopped
- 150 g Celery, cut into 2cm lengths

- 1 tsp Mild curry powder
- 130 g Tomato, cut into 8 wedges
- 100 ml Chicken or vegetable stock
- 1 tbsp Chopped parsley

Method

\# Heat the oven to 200C / gas mark 6.

\# Start with the spicy celery. Heat a frying pan over a medium–low heat, add the olive oil, then the onion, garlic, ginger, chilli and celery. Fry gently for 2–3 minutes or until softened but not coloured, then add the curry powder and cook for a further minute.

\# Add the tomatoes then the stock and lentils and simmer gently for 10 minutes. You may want to increase or decrease the cooking time depending on how crunchy you like your celery.

Meanwhile, mix the turmeric, oil and lemon juice and rub over the salmon. # Place on a baking tray and cook for 8–10 minutes.

To finish, stir the parsley through the celery and serve with the salmon.

sirtfood recipesCORONATION CHICKEN SALAD-SIRTFOOD RECIPES

Serves 1

Preparation time: 5 minutes

Ingredients

- 75 g Natural yoghurt
- Juice of 1/4 of a lemon
- 1 tsp Coriander, chopped
- 1 tsp Ground turmeric

- 1/2 tsp Mild curry powder
- 100 g Cooked chicken breast, cut into bite-sized pieces
- 6 Walnut halves, finely chopped
- 1 Medjool date, finely chopped
- 20 g Red onion, diced
- 1 Bird's eye chilli
- 40 g Rocket, to serve

Method

Mix the yoghurt, lemon juice, coriander and spices together in a bowl. Add all the remaining ingredients and serve on a bed of the rocket.

BAKED POTATOES WITH SPICY CHICKPEA STEW- SIRTFOOD RECIPESsirtfood recipes

Prep time

10 mins

Cook time

1 hour

Serves 4-6

Kind of Mexican Mole meets North African Tagine, this Spicy Chickpea Stew is unbelievably delicious and makes a great topping for baked potatoes, plus it just happens to be vegetarian, vegan, gluten free and dairy free. And it contains chocolate.

Ingredients

- 4-6 baking potatoes, pricked all over
- 2 tablespoons olive oil
- 2 red onions, finely chopped
- 4 cloves garlic, grated or crushed
- 2cm ginger, grated
- ½ -2 teaspoons chilli flakes (depending on how hot you like things)
- 2 tablespoons cumin seeds
- 2 tablespoons turmeric
- Splash of water
- 2 x 400g tins chopped tomatoes
- 2 tablespoons unsweetened cocoa powder (or cacao)
- 2 x 400g tins chickpeas (or kidney beans if you prefer) including the chickpea water DON'T DRAIN!!

- 2 yellow peppers (or whatever colour you prefer!), chopped into bitesize pieces
- 2 tablespoons parsley plus extra for garnish
- Salt and pepper to taste (optional)
- Side salad (optional)

Method

1. Preheat the oven to 200C, meanwhile you can prepare all your ingredients.

2. When the oven is hot enough put your baking potatoes in the oven and cook for 1 hour or until they are done how you like them.

3. Once the potatoes are in the oven, place the olive oil and chopped red onion in a large wide saucepan and

cook gently, with the lid on for 5 minutes, until the onions are soft but not brown.

4.Remove the lid and add the garlic, ginger, cumin and chilli. Cook for a further minute on a low heat, then add the turmeric and a very small splash of water and cook for another minute, taking care not to let the pan get too dry.

5.Next, add in the tomatoes, cocoa powder (or cacao), chickpeas (including the chickpea water) and yellow pepper. Bring to the boil, then simmer on a low heat for 45 minutes until the sauce is thick and unctuous (but don't let it burn!). The stew should be done at roughly the same time as the potatoes.

6.Finally stir in the 2 tablespoons of parsley, and some salt and pepper if you wish, and serve the stew on top of the baked potatoes, perhaps with a simple side salad.

GRAPE AND MELON JUICE – SIRTFOOD RECIPES

125 calories

2 of your SIRT 5 a day

Serves 1 • Ready in 2 minutes

- ½ cucumber, peeled if preferred, halved, seeds removed and roughly chopped
- 30g young spinach leaves, stalks removed
- 100g red seedless grapes
- 100g cantaloupe melon, peeled, deseeded and cut into chunks
- 1 Blend together in a juicer or blender until smooth.

KALE AND RED ONION DHAL WITH BUCKWHEAT-SIRTFOOD RECIPESsirtfood recipes

Prep time

5 mins

Cook time

25 mins

Total time

30 mins

Serves:4

Delicious and very nutritious this Kale and Red Onion Dhal with Buckwheat is quick and easy to make and naturally gluten free, dairy free, vegetarian and vegan.

INGREDIENTS

- 1 tablespoon olive oil
- 1 small red onion, sliced
- 3 garlic cloves, grated or crushed
- 2 cm ginger, grated
- 1 birds eye chilli, deseeded and finely chopped (more if you like things hot!)
- 2 teaspoons turmeric
- 2 teaspoons garam masala
- 160g red lentils
- 400ml coconut milk
- 200ml water
- 100g kale (or spinach would be a great alternative)
- 160g buckwheat (or brown rice)

METHOD

1. Put the olive oil in a large, deep saucepan and add the sliced onion. Cook on a low heat, with the lid on for 5 minutes until softened.

2. Add the garlic, ginger and chilli and cook for 1 more minute.

3. Add the turmeric, garam masala and a splash of water and cook for 1 more minute.

4. Add the red lentils, coconut milk, and 200ml water (do this simply by half filling the coconut milk can with water and tipping it into the saucepan).

5. Mix everything together thoroughly and cook for 20 minutes over a gently heat with the lid on. Stir occasionally and add a little more water if the dhal starts to stick.

6. After 20 minutes add the kale, stir thoroughly and replace the lid, cook for a further 5 minutes (1-2 minutes if you use spinach instead!)

7. About 15 minutes before the curry is ready, place the buckwheat in a medium saucepan and add plenty of boiling water. Bring the water back to the boil and cook for 10 minutes (or a little longer if you prefer your buckwheat softer. Drain the buckwheat in a sieve and serve with the dhal.

sirtfood recipes

CHARGRILLED BEEF WITH A RED WINE JUS, ONION RINGS, GARLIC KALE AND HERB ROASTED POTATOES- SIRTFOOD RECIPES

INGREDIENTS:

- 100g potatoes, peeled and cut into 2cm dice

- 1 tbsp extra virgin olive oil
- 5g parsley, finely chopped
- 50g red onion, sliced into rings
- 50g kale, sliced
- 1 garlic clove, finely chopped
- 120–150g x 3.5cm-thick beef fillet steak or 2cm-thick sirloin steak
- 40ml red wine
- 150ml beef stock
- 1 tsp tomato purée
- 1 tsp cornflour, dissolved in 1 tbsp water

INSTRUCTIONS:

Heat the oven to 220ºC/gas 7.

Place the potatoes in a saucepan of boiling water, bring back to the boil and cook for 4–5 minutes, then drain.

Place in a roasting tin with 1 teaspoon of the oil and roast in the hot oven for 35–45 minutes. Turn the potatoes every 10 minutes to ensure even cooking. When cooked, remove from the oven, sprinkle with the chopped parsley and mix well. Fry the onion in 1 teaspoon of the oil over a medium heat for 5–7 minutes, until soft and nicely caramelised. Keep warm. Steam the kale for 2–3 minutes then drain. Fry the garlic gently in ½ teaspoon of oil for 1 minute, until soft but not coloured. Add the kale and fry for a further 1–2 minutes, until tender. Keep warm.

Heat an ovenproof frying pan over a high heat until smoking. Coat the meat in ½ a teaspoon of the oil and fry in the hot pan over a medium–high heat according to how you like your meat done. If you like your meat medium it would be better to sear the meat and then transfer the pan to an oven set at 220ºC/gas 7 and finish the cooking that way for the prescribed times. Remove the meat from the pan and set aside to rest. Add the wine to the hot pan to bring up any meat residue. Bubble to reduce the wine by half, until syrupy and with a concentrated flavor. Add the stock and tomato purée to the steak pan and bring to the boil, then add the cornflour paste to thicken your sauce, adding it a little at a time until you have your desired consistency. Stir in any of the juices from the rested steak and serve with the roasted potatoes, kale, onion rings and red wine sauce.

KALE AND BLACKCURRANT SMOOTHIE-SIRTFOOD RECIPES

sirtfood diet recipes

86 calories

1 – 1/2 of your SIRT 5 a day

Serves 2 • Ready in 3 minutes

- 2 tsp honey
- 1 cup freshly made green tea
- 10 baby kale leaves, stalks removed
- 1 ripe banana
- 40 g blackcurrants, washed and stalks removed
- 6 ice cubes

Stir the honey into the warm green tea until dissolved. Whiz all the ingredients together in a blender until smooth. Serve immediately.

BUCKWHEAT PASTA SALAD-SIRTFOOD RECIPES

Serves 1

- 50g buckwheat pasta(cooked according to the packet instructions)sirtfood recipes
- large handful of rocket
- small handful of basil leaves
- 8 cherry tomatoes,halved
- 1/2 avocado,diced
- 10 olives
- 1 tbsp extra virgin olive oil
- 20g pine nuts

Gently combine all the ingredients except the pine nuts and arrange on a plate or in a bowl,then scatter the pine nuts over the top.

GREEK SALAD SKEWERS-SIRTFOOD RECIPESsirtfood recipes

306 calories • 3.5 of your SIRT 5 a day

Serves 2 • Ready in 10 minutes

- 2 wooden skewers, soaked in water for 30 minutes before use

- 8 large black olives

- 8 cherry tomatoes

- 1 yellow pepper, cut into 8 squares

- ½ red onion, cut in half and separated into 8 pieces

- 100g (about 10cm) cucumber, cut into 4 slices and halved

- 100g feta, cut into 8 cubes

- For the dressing:

- 1 tbsp extra virgin olive oil

- Juice of ½ lemon

- 1 tsp balsamic vinegar

- ½ clove garlic, peeled and crushed

- Few leaves basil, finely chopped (or ½ tsp dried mixed herbs to replace basil and oregano)

- Few leaves oregano, finely chopped

- Generous seasoning of salt and freshly ground black pepper

1 Thread each skewer with the salad ingredients in the order: olive, tomato, yellow pepper, red onion, cucumber, feta, tomato, olive, yellow pepper, red onion, cucumber, feta.

2 Place all the dressing ingredients in a small bowl and mix together thoroughly. Pour over the skewers.

KALE, EDAMAME AND TOFU CURRY-SIRTFOOD RECIPES sirtfood recipes

- 342 calories

- 2 1/2 of your SIRT 5 a day

- A warming and wintry curry. Easy to keep either refrigerated or frozen for another day.

Serves 4 • Ready in 45 minutes

- 1 tbsp rapeseed oil
- 1 large onion, chopped
- 4 cloves garlic, peeled and grated
- 1 large thumb (7cm) fresh ginger, peeled and grated
- 1 red chilli, deseeded and thinly sliced
- 1/2 tsp ground turmeric
- 1/4 tsp cayenne pepper
- 1 tsp paprika
- 1/2 tsp ground cumin
- 1 tsp salt
- 250g dried red lentils
- 1 litre boiling water
- 50g frozen soyaedamame beans
- 200g firm tofu, chopped into cubes
- 2 tomatoes, roughly chopped
- Juice of 1 lime

- 200g kale leaves, stalks removed and torn

1 Put the oil in a heavy-bottomed pan over a low-medium heat. Add the onion and cook for 5 minutes before adding the garlic, ginger and chilli and cooking for a further 2 minutes. Add the turmeric, cayenne, paprika, cumin and salt. Stir through before adding the red lentils and stirring again.

2 Pour in the boiling water and bring to a hearty simmer for 10 minutes, then reduce the heat and cook for a further 20-30 minutes until the curry has a thick '•porridge' consistency.

3 Add the soya beans, tofu and tomatoes and cook for a further 5 minutes. Add the lime juice and kale leaves and cook until the kale is just tender.

CHOCOLATE CUPCAKES WITH MATCHA ICING- SIRTFOOD RECIPESsirtfood recipes

234 calories • 1 of your SIRT 5 a day

Simply awesome!

MAKES 12 • READY IN 35 MINUTES

- 150g self-raising flour

- 200g caster sugar

- 60g cocoa

- ½ tsp salt

- ½ tsp fine espresso coffee, decaf if preferred

- 120ml milk

- ½ tsp vanilla extract

- 50ml vegetable oil

- 1 egg

- 120ml boiling water

- For the icing:

- 50g butter, at room temperature

- 50g icing sugar

- 1 tbsp matcha green tea powder

- ½ tsp vanilla bean paste

- 50g soft cream cheese

- Preheat the oven to 180C/160C fan. Line a cupcake tin with paper or silicone cake cases.

- Place the flour, sugar, cocoa, salt and espresso powder in a large bowl and mix thoroughly.

- Add the milk, vanilla extract, vegetable oil and egg to the dry ingredients and use an electric mixer to beat until well combined. Carefully pour in the boiling water slowly and beat on a low speed until fully combined. Use a high speed to beat for a further minute to add air to the batter. The batter is much more liquid than a normal cake mix. Have faith, it will taste amazing!

- Spoon the batter evenly between the cake cases. Each cake case should be no more than ¾ full. Bake in the oven for 15-18 minutes, until the mixture bounces back when tapped. Remove from the oven and allow to cool completely before icing.

- To make the icing, cream the butter and icing sugar together until it's pale and smooth. Add the matcha powder and vanilla and stir again. Finally add the cream cheese and beat until smooth. Pipe or spread over the cakes.

CONCLUSION

The Sirtfood Diet is full of healthy foods, but not healthy eating patterns. Adding some sirtfoods to your diet is not a bad idea and it even offer many health benefits, the diet itself is health and seeks to better improve the overall health of the human body.

CPSIA information can be obtained
at www.ICGtesting.com
Printed in the USA
LVHW081118180721
693016LV00019B/479